Industrial Giants

Debra J. Housel, M.S.Ed.

Publishing Credits

Historical Consultant
Jeff Burke, M.Ed.

Editors
Wendy Conklin, M.A.
Torrey Maloof

Editorial Director
Emily R. Smith, M.A.Ed.

Editor-in-Chief
Sharon Coan, M.S.Ed.

Creative Director
Lee Aucoin

Illustration Manager
Timothy J. Bradley

Publisher
Rachelle Cracchiolo, M.S.Ed.

Teacher Created Materials
5301 Oceanus Drive
Huntington Beach, CA 92649-1030
http://www.tcmpub.com

ISBN 978-0-7439-0661-6

Printed in China
Nordica.082019.CA21901100

Table of Contents

When Industry Began

By the early 1800s, America had machines and factories. Yet, many things were still made by hand. After the Civil War, things changed. Railroads spread across the nation. Goods could move more easily. Machines became more important.

Inventors created new items. Then, businesses recreated them in great quantities. Bankers lent money to help companies grow. By the 1900s, big businesses sold oil, steel, and cars.

Natural resources played a part, too. Forests provided lumber. Rivers offered water power. Miners brought coal and iron ore out of the ground. These are the materials needed for steel. Steel was used to build machines, bridges, railroad tracks, and cars. Oil from underground was changed in **refineries** (rih-FINE-uh-reez). Then, it could be used to run cars and machines.

The fastest growth occurred in the North. This change came about because of powerful men. Together they created an **economy** (ih-KAWN-uh-mee) that was the envy of the world.

Men repair steel railroad tracks in 1863.

Lumbermen use a steam locomotive to move huge logs.

In 1888, men work with large machines inside a sawmill.

Fast-Paced Growth

At one time, the United States depended on other countries for goods. By 1890, the country could produce almost everything it needed!

Sweatshops

The rise of factories was not free of problems. Many people, including young children, worked in bad conditions. They had long hours in hot, dirty, and dangerous locations. These places were called **sweatshops**.

A child works in a sweatshop in Virginia.

Sleepy Travelers

Although trains were the fastest way to travel at the time, it could take days to get someplace. People needed to sleep while they rode the train. That's why sleeping cars made a lot of money for railroad investors.

Owning a Company

People could buy stock in a company. A person gave the business owner money in return for stock. It stated that the person owned a small part of the business and would get a small part of the profits. The more stock a person held, the more he owned of the company.

Four men sleep while traveling across country on a train.

Stock certificate from the late nineteenth century

A Man of Steel

Andrew Carnegie was 12 years old when he came to the United States in 1847. His family had no money. His father had lost his job in Scotland. From the start, Carnegie had to work. He delivered telegrams. He soon taught himself how to use a telegraph machine. At that time, it was the fastest way to send a message.

When Carnegie was 17 years old, a rail **executive** (ig-ZEK-yuh-tiv) noticed him. The executive kept Carnegie working with him as he moved up the chain of command. He also lent Carnegie money. Carnegie took the money and invested in the Woodruff Sleeping Car Company. This company made sleeping cars for trains.

Carnegie also bought **stock** in the Keystone Bridge Company. Keystone built iron train bridges. These two **investments** gave Carnegie a good income at a young age. He would soon use that money to make an even better investment in steel.

ANDREW CARNEGIE
1861

There is a telegraph line next to this railroad that is being built.

Mr. and Mrs. Carnegie in 1908

Henry Frick

An Original Thinker

Carnegie became involved in running the Pennsylvania Railroad. He knew that the trains must keep moving or goods would spoil. He would even set fire to stalled cars to get them off the tracks! This is just one example of the kind of outside-the-box thinking that Carnegie did. This kind of thinking made him very successful. He became one of the richest men in America.

Carnegie left the railroad business in 1865. He started his own business. He opened a big modern steel mill. He was smart enough to make correct guesses about what the future would bring. So even when the economy dipped, his company kept growing.

Carnegie bought out other steel mills. Then he bought a **coke** company. This company's owner, Henry Frick, became Carnegie's partner.

A 5'3" Blonde Takes Charge

Other business leaders towered over the short blonde Carnegie. But Carnegie was smart, hard working, forceful, and decisive. No one who met him ever forgot him.

Don't Drink This Coke!

Coke is a solid fuel made by heating coal in the absence of air. It fueled blast furnaces in steel-making plants. These furnaces separate iron ore into iron and steel. This is very different than the drink you know of as Coke® today!

This painting gives an inside look at one of Carnegie's steel factories.

Strike!

In 1892, Carnegie went on vacation to Scotland. While he was gone, his steel workers went on **strike**. That means they stopped working. Their pay had been cut with their new contracts. Carnegie wanted to pay them more, but Henry Frick did not. He did not like **union** workers. Frick tried to open the plant by force. The strikers attacked some guards at the mill. Some people died. The National Guard had to be called in to help. Carnegie had said that he believed in workers' rights. But in this case, he did not step in to help the workers. Many people felt Carnegie could have prevented this crisis.

In 1901, Carnegie sold the Carnegie Steel Company for $480 million. Then he retired.

There were many strikes during this time period. This strike occurred in New York City ten years after the steel workers' strike at Carnegie's mill.

Labor Unions

A labor union is a group of workers. This group stands up to the boss if the company does not give them better working conditions or fair pay. By joining together, they make a difference. The company knows that if the workers go on strike, the factory does not produce.

A Historic First

J. P. Morgan bought Carnegie Steel. He combined it with other companies to form U.S. Steel. This was the first business in the world to be worth one billion dollars.

J. P. Morgan

The strike at Carnegie's steel mill became violent. Many people were hurt.

A Big Saver

In 1839, John D. Rockefeller was born on a farm in New York State. Even as a child, he had a good mind for business. At the age of seven, he found a wild turkey's nest. When the chicks were big enough to leave the nest, he took them home. He fed them for a few weeks. Then he sold them. He put the money in a jar. That was the beginning of his savings.

Rockefeller worked for a farmer for 35 cents a day. By the age of 10, Rockefeller had $50 in his money jar. A man asked to borrow the money. He told Rockefeller that he would pay **interest**. After a year, Rockefeller received $53.50 back from the man. At that moment, he knew that he would go into business. But, he had no idea that he would become one of the richest men of his time.

John D. Rockefeller Jr. built Rockefeller Center in New York City during the Great Depression.

John D. Rockefeller in 1910

Saving Money

It was amazing that Rockefeller saved $50 by the age of 10. In 1849, the average weekly pay for adults was less than $5. Rockefeller only earned $.35 a day. How many days did he work to save that much money?

How Interest Works

Interest is a fee paid when you borrow money. Rockefeller earned $3.50 in interest. That's 7% percent of the original $50. That's not a bad rate of interest even today!

As a child, Rockefeller did not put his money in a bank. He kept it in a jar!

Refining Crude Oil

Oil cannot be used directly out of the ground. It must be broken down into parts. A refinery separates crude oil into gasoline, fuel oil, kerosene, and diesel. Then, it can be sold to people.

Muckraker Ida Tarbell

A **muckraker** was a person who wrote about problems in society. Ida Tarbell wrote a book that claimed Rockefeller was a cheater. It increased public distrust of him. From that point on, he slept with a gun. He felt he needed to protect himself.

Ida Tarbell

Crude oil is separated using chemicals or different temperatures.

Oil gushing from the ground in Texas

Getting Started in Oil

Rockefeller got his education at a time when many children did not go to school. He learned to be a bookkeeper. He saved his money and found two partners. When he was 22, he had saved enough money to help build Excelsior (ik-SELL-see-or) Oil Company. The company drilled oil. The company had a good refinery. The refinery was near rail and water transportation. This would help him transport his oil.

Excelsior became the best, most modern American refinery. After just three years, Rockefeller bought his partners' stock in the company. That meant he owned the whole company.

In 1870, he and some new partners started the Standard Oil Company. It was soon the world's biggest refinery. The refinery was very efficient. It saved time and money. The cost of refining oil lowered. But, the money still poured in from consumers. Rockefeller used his money to buy other refineries, oil fields, oil tank cars, and pipelines.

A 1913 Standard Oil Company plant in California

Wise Businessman or Robber Baron?

By 1879, Standard Oil controlled almost all of America's oil business. The company then created **trusts**. The trusts made competitors limit how much oil they could produce. The competitors were also forced to keep their prices low. People did not like the fact that Standard Oil told everyone what to do. They called Rockefeller and others like him "robber barons." Robber barons were people who got rich through **shady** business deals.

This political cartoon shows Standard Oil as an octopus taking control over everything in the United States.

Rockefeller takes a walk with his son. John D. Rockefeller Jr. was a director at Standard Oil.

America's First Billionaire

Rockefeller was the first American billionaire. At the time of his death in 1937, his fortune was $1.4 billion. That's about $13 billion in today's dollars!

Let's Play Monopoly

The game Monopoly® was created in 1934. The goal of the game is to buy more property than anyone else. That way, one player can monopolize, or control, the board.

Monopoly® allows people to feel the power of being robber barons!

Just a few years later, the Sherman Antitrust Act was passed by Congress. This act made it against the law to limit other people's businesses. The act also did not allow **monopolies** (muh-NAWP-uh-leez). A monopoly is when one company controls a whole industry. Rockefeller tried to get around these laws. The U.S. Supreme Court stopped him. However, Rockefeller had already made his fortune.

Born to Be a Banker

The Risk of Banking

Bankers lose money if they lend funds to businesses that fail or to a person who cannot pay. That is why it was so important that Morgan recognized good risks.

Draft Dodger

Morgan was drafted to fight in the Civil War. However, he did not go. He paid a poor man $300 to take his place. Many rich men did this during the Civil War.

The Civil War lasted from 1861–1865.

Banks during the Industrial **Revolution** (rev-uh-LOO-shuhn) were similar to banks today. People saved their money. Then, they took it to a bank. Banks gave people an interest rate of about one percent. If a person put $1,000 in the bank, a year later the bank would owe that person $1,010.

The banks stored the money. Banks also lent out money to other people. Those people had to pay back the banks. However, these people had to give back the original amount plus three percent interest. So if they borrowed $1,000, they had to pay back $1,030. The banks made profits from lending money. The profit is the difference between the interest earned and the interest paid. For this $1,000, the bank earned a profit of $30.

John Pierpont (J. P.) Morgan was born in 1837. His father was a banker. When Morgan grew up, he worked for his father. He soon knew the banking business inside and out. He struck out on his own in 1862. He had a knack for knowing which businesses would grow. He made sure he lent money to those businesses.

J. P. Morgan was a smart banker. He became very successful. This is him in 1902.

This is the J. P. Morgan & Company building on the corner of Wall and Broad streets in 1914. It is still in New York City today.

A Powerful Man

Morgan became the main **financier** (fih-nan-SUHR) for General Electric and other large companies. That means he loaned these companies a lot of money. He also provided funds for the railroads. At the height of his career, he controlled banks, railroads, insurance companies, and shipping lines. He was so powerful that some people even thought that he wanted to take control of the whole country.

Morgan had a bad temper. He threw food at his servants. He did not care what others thought of him. He also ignored business laws. Once, his lawyer told him that what he wanted to do was not legal. Morgan snapped, "I know that. I asked you to find out how to make it legal." Yet, people in Europe trusted him. They gave him money to invest. He used it to build American businesses.

Morgan financed the American Telegraph and Telephone Company. This company is known as AT&T today.

Morgan bought both American and European shipping companies.

These Russian farmers use tractors made in the United States.

Capital Means Money

The word **capital** means the same thing as money. Capital was important to the rise of industry. Natural resources and machinery were important, too. Financiers such as Morgan developed large industries to make capital.

International Harvester

A company called International Harvester made equipment used to plant and harvest crops. It made plows, tractors, and other farm equipment. These machines helped farmers to grow more crops than ever before in history.

Making a Monopoly

In the late 1800s, people had paper money that could be traded for gold. In 1895, the economy slowed down. People worried. They started to demand gold payments for their paper money. The U.S. Treasury did not have enough gold to cover all the paper money. So, it asked Morgan for help. He sold 62 million dollars in gold-backed bonds. This stopped a national panic.

In 1901, Morgan created the Northern Securities Company. It controlled the railroads in the West. This created a monopoly. But, he did not think that the United States government would try to stop him. After all, he had saved the U.S. economy in 1895.

In 1902 President Theodore Roosevelt took action. He knew that Morgan's business **violated** (VYE-uh-late-uhd) the Sherman Antitrust Act. The case went before the U.S. Supreme Court. The court ended Morgan's monopoly.

The Panic of 1895

In 1895, Morgan kept the U.S. government from collapsing! The United States was running out of gold. Morgan's group sold people gold-backed bonds. Americans and Europeans who trusted Morgan provided this gold. By June, the United States had restored its gold reserves.

Holding a Grudge

Morgan never forgave President Roosevelt for ending his railroad monopoly. When the president went on an African safari, Morgan publicly stated, "I hope a lion will eat him!"

President Theodore Roosevelt helped the government control the robber barons.

Many Americans did not like that Morgan and his associates controlled America's railways.

This poster shows Americans running to take their money out of failing banks. Morgan saved the banks with his gold-backed bonds.

The Car Maker

Henry Ford was born in Dearborn, Michigan, in 1863. As a child, he loved tools and engines. As a teen, he fixed watches. At age 16, Ford walked to Detroit. He took a job at a machine shop. Then, he went to work for the biggest shipbuilder in the city. There he learned all about motors.

Ford wanted to build a gas engine. In 1891, he told his wife that he would build a "horseless carriage." She never doubted him. He took a job with Thomas Edison so he could learn about electricity.

In 1903, Ford and two partners formed Ford Motor Company. They started to make cars. But the cars cost a lot. Only very rich people could afford to buy them. In 1908, Ford brought out the Model T. This car was very popular and less expensive than other cars. More than 10,000 were sold the first year.

Cars were put together on assembly lines at Ford Motor Company.

Henry Ford appeared on the cover of *TIME* magazine in January 1935.

Always Up to Something

Ford was bright, but he did not like school. He always wanted to be making something. Each day during recess, he and a friend worked on building a steam engine. Then they tried to run it. It blew up and set the school's fence on fire!

King Car

Many important inventions—including the electric light, the telephone, and the typewriter—appeared in the late 1800s. The invention of the car had the biggest impact on people's lifestyles and the country's economy.

The Ford Model T was a very popular car.

Fast Assembly

In 1912, it took 12.5 hours to make one car. The assembly line sped things up. Just two years later, in 1914 it took only 1.5 hours to make a Model T.

Standardized Parts

Model T cars had many parts. To get the cars put together right, Ford had to standardize the parts. That means that every Model T had exactly the same wheels, doors, and other parts. The combination of the assembly line and standardized parts made it possible to make more cars quickly.

The Assembly Line Is Born

The Ford Motor Company could not keep up with the demand. That gave Ford an idea. He invented the **assembly line**. Men stood along a **conveyor belt** (kuhn-VAY-uhr belt). As an engine moved past, each worker did one job. One man placed a bolt. Another man put on the nut. A third man tightened it. This sped up the process of building a car.

In 1914, most employers gave poor pay for long hours. Ford wanted to change this and reward his workers. He doubled their pay and cut their hours. This was shocking.

Ford Motor Company started making all of its own parts. Then Ford had another new idea. Parts cost less to ship than cars. So, he sent car parts to other cities. There, workers put them together. As the cost to make a car dropped, he cut the price. A $1,000 car in 1905 cost just $290 by 1924. Most people could now buy one! The era of the car had arrived.

These assembly line workers are making wheels.

Men working at the Ford Motor Plant in 1900. They are building the car by hand.

Assembly lines are still used to make cars today.

Giving Away Money

Each of these rich **industrialists** (in-DUHS-tree-uhl-istz) used some of his fortune to help others. These men left **foundations** with so much money that they still exist today. Andrew Carnegie built over 2,500 public libraries. He also started Carnegie Mellon University. And he gave funds for research in science.

John D. Rockefeller funded Rockefeller University. It had the first American medical lab. He started the Rockefeller Foundation, too. It gives money to improve medicine, farming, and education.

During his life, J. P. Morgan gave money to churches, hospitals, and schools. When he died, he left his art collection to the Metropolitan Museum of Art. It is in New York City.

In 1935, Henry Ford and his son set up the Ford Foundation. It gives money for education and research. He also started Greenfield Village and the Henry Ford Museum. Both are in his hometown of Dearborn, Michigan.

The Metropolitan Museum of Art is located in New York City.

Carnegie Mellon University

Racecars like this Ford GT Mark IV are displayed at the Henry Ford Museum.

The Gospel of Wealth

Carnegie said, "The man who dies with his fortune still intact dies disgraced." He wanted to encourage wealthy men to give their money to good causes. This is called **philanthropy** (fuh-LAN-thruh-pee).

Greenfield Village

This was the first historical village in the United States. Ford bought old buildings and had them moved to the village. He wanted future generations to see how people lived at the turn of the century.

Greenfield Village gives a glimpse into the past.

Glossary

assembly line—an arrangement of workers where an item moves along a conveyer belt and workers add to the item as it moves along until the whole piece is assembled

capital—money; often used to start a business

coke—a solid fuel made by heating coal in the absence of air

conveyor belt—a continuously moving band that transports things from one point to another

economy—the way a nation runs its industry, trade, and finance

executive—a person with an important, powerful job in a company

financier—a person who lends funds to organizations to make a profit

foundations—organizations that give away money to worthwhile causes

industrialists—people who own or control manufacturing businesses

interest—a fee paid for borrowing money

investments—properties or possessions purchased for future income or benefit

monopolies—total control of markets or industries

muckraker—a person who writes about corruption in society to try to change laws

philanthropy—the act of giving money away to benefit others

refineries—factories where crude oil is purified and made into finished products such as gasoline, propane, diesel, and kerosene

revolution—to cause change or reform in the way things are done

shady—not trustworthy

stock—a share in a company that shows ownership and a right to receive part of the profits

strike—to stop working until an agreement is made between workers and owners

sweatshops—businesses with poor working conditions; workers were often children and women

trusts—arrangements in which people (trustees) hold or use property for the benefit of others

union—an organization of workers formed to promote improved wages and working conditions

violated—broke a law, rule, or promise

Index

Image Credits

cover The Library of Congress; p.1 The Library of Congress; p.4 The Library of Congress; p.5 (top left) The Library of Congress; p.5 (bottom left) The Library of Congress; p.5 (right) The Library of Congress; p.6 (top) Fox Photos/Hulton Archive/Getty Images; p.6 (bottom) Robert O. Brown Photography/Shutterstock, Inc.; p.7 (top) The Library of Congress; p.7 (bottom) Bettmann/Corbis; p.8 (left) The Library of Congress; p.8 (right) The Library of Congress; p.9 The Granger Collection, New York; p.10 The Library of Congress; pp.10–11 The Library of Congress; p.11 The Library of Congress; p.12 The Library of Congress; p.13 (top) The Library of Congress; p.13 (bottom) Joshua Williams/Shutterstock, Inc.; p.14 (top) Photos.com; p.14 (left bottom) The Library of Congress; p.14 (right bottom) The Library of Congress; p.15 The Library of Congress; pp.16–17 The Library of Congress; p.17 (left) The Library of Congress; p.17 (right) Nikolay Okhitin/Dreamstime.com; p.18 The Library of Congress; p.19 (top) The Library of Congress; p.19 (bottom) The Library of Congress; p.20 Bettmann/Corbis; p.21 (top) The Library of Congress; p.21 (bottom) Underwood & Underwood/Corbis; p.22 Photos.com; p.23 (top) The Library of Congress; p.23 (bottom) The Library of Congress; p.24 The Library of Congress; p.25 (top) Time & Life Pictures/Getty Images; p.25 (bottom) Julio Yeste/Shutterstock, Inc.; p.26 Stringer/Hulton Archive/Getty Images; p.27 (top) Archive Holdings Inc./Getty Images; p.27 (bottom) Sandy Felsenthal/Corbis; p.28 Bob Krist/Corbis; p.29 (top) Richard Cummins/Corbis; p.29 (left bottom) Directphoto.org/Alamy; p.29 (right bottom) Stephen Saks Photography/Alamy